Mystic Mountain Christmas

ISBN:9781717571922

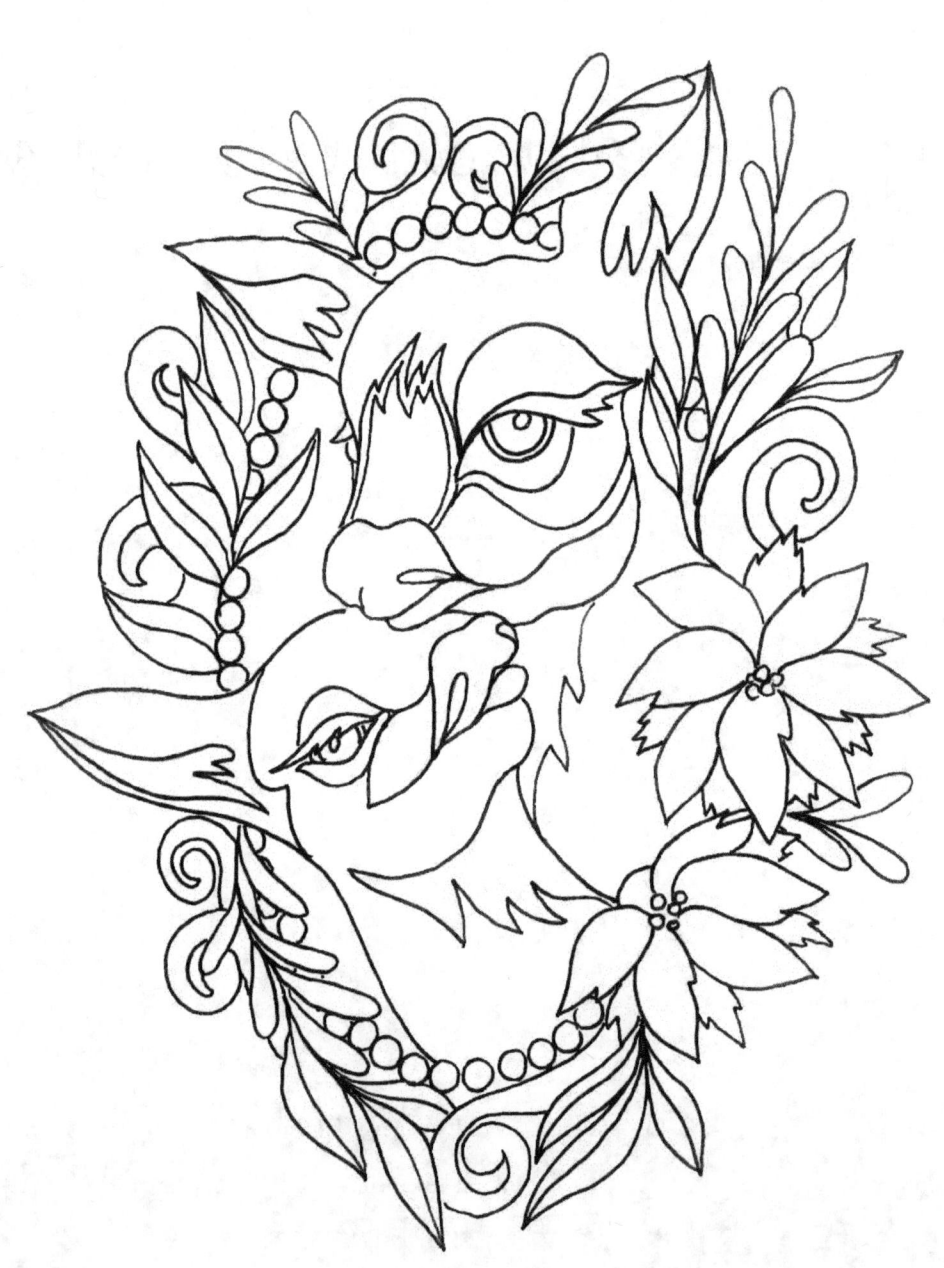

Fawn Love

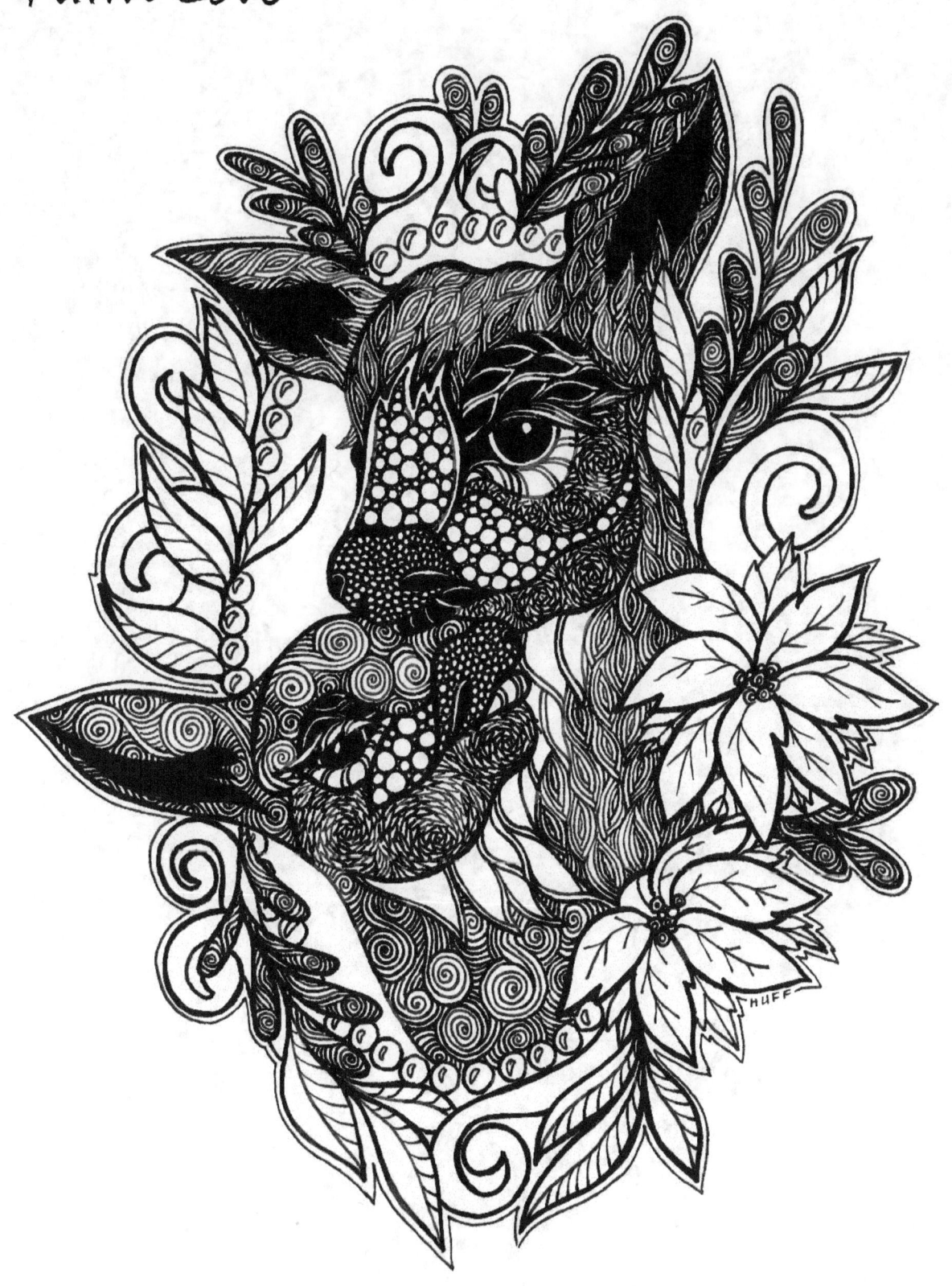

Singing Chickadees

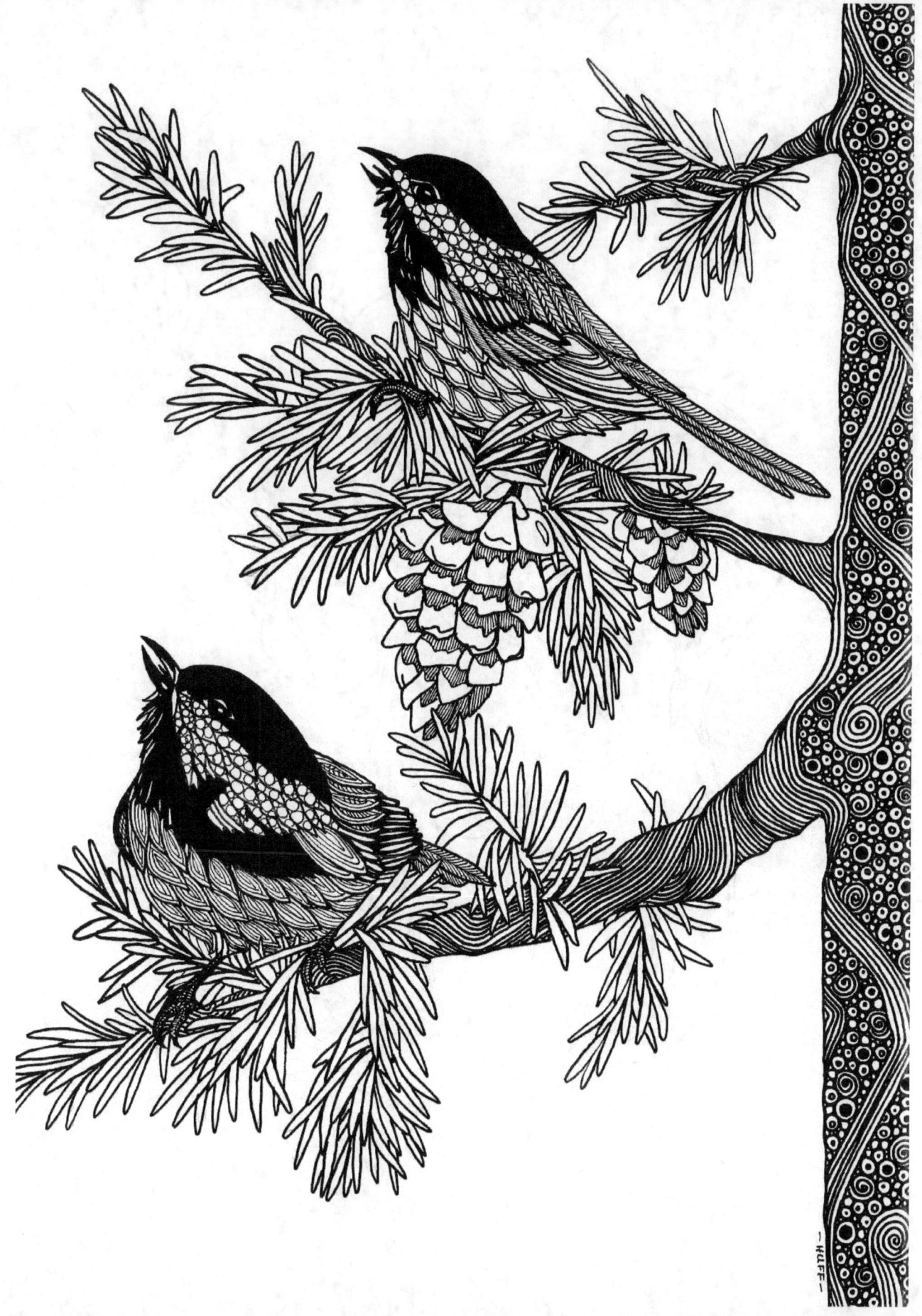

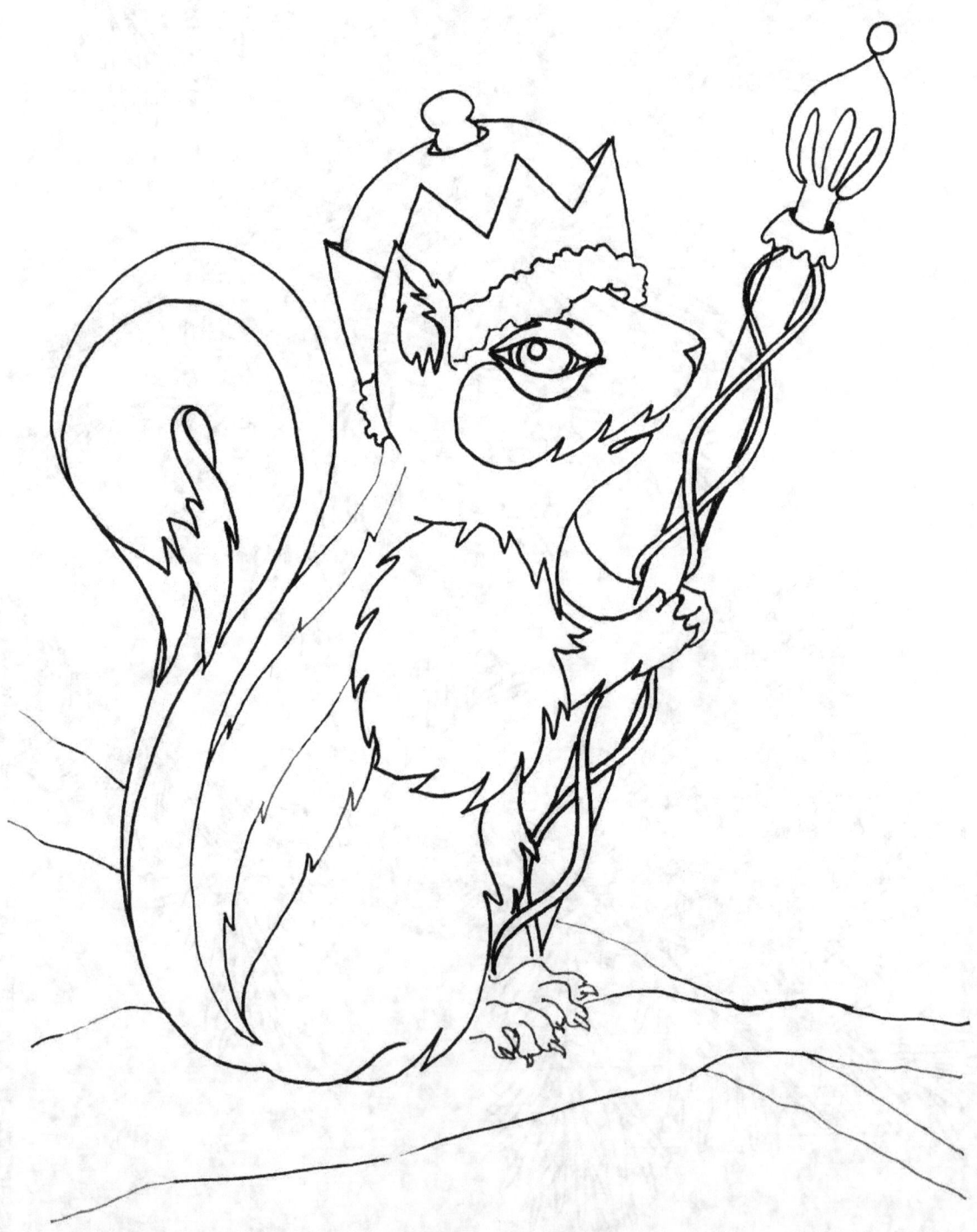

Nutcracker

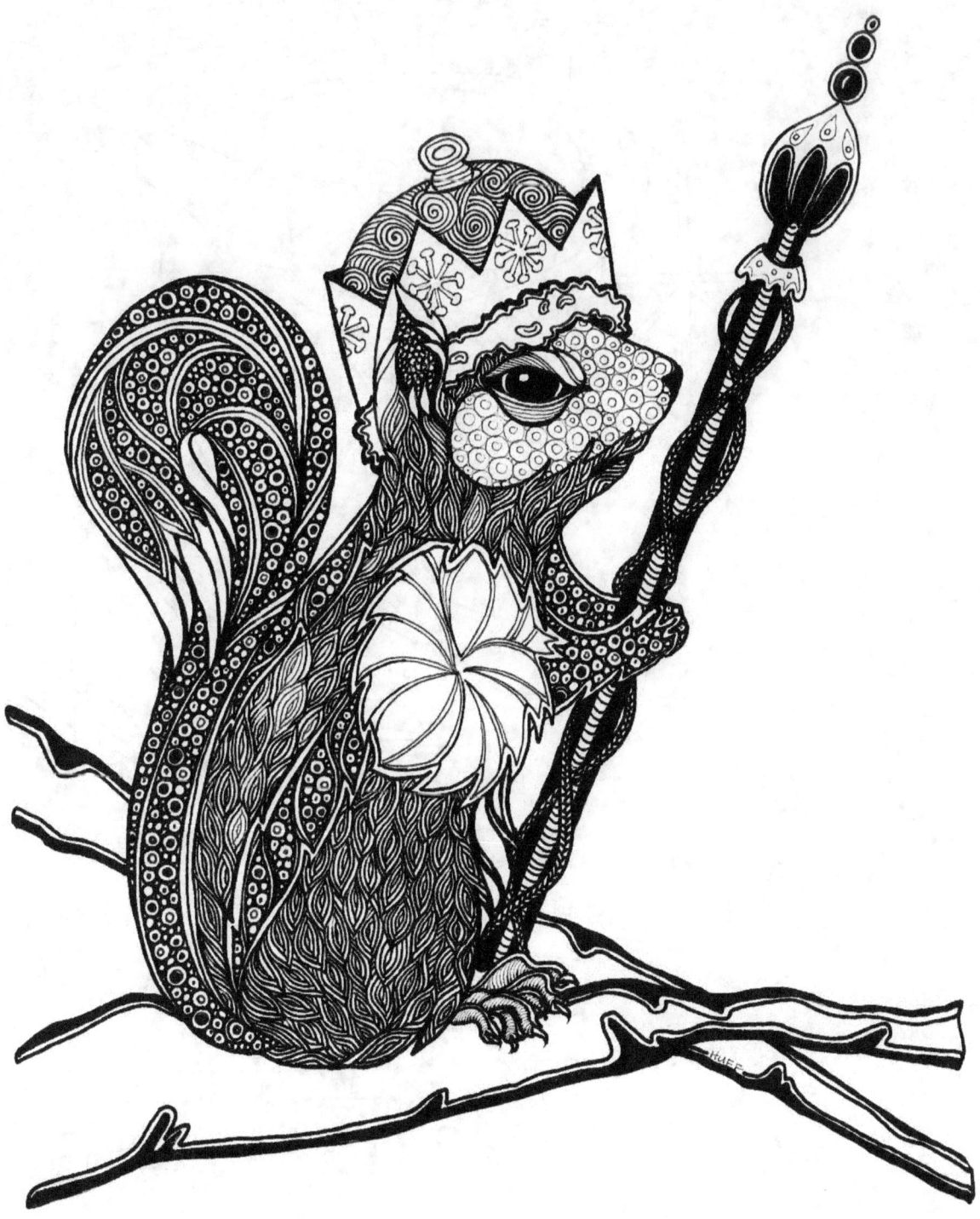

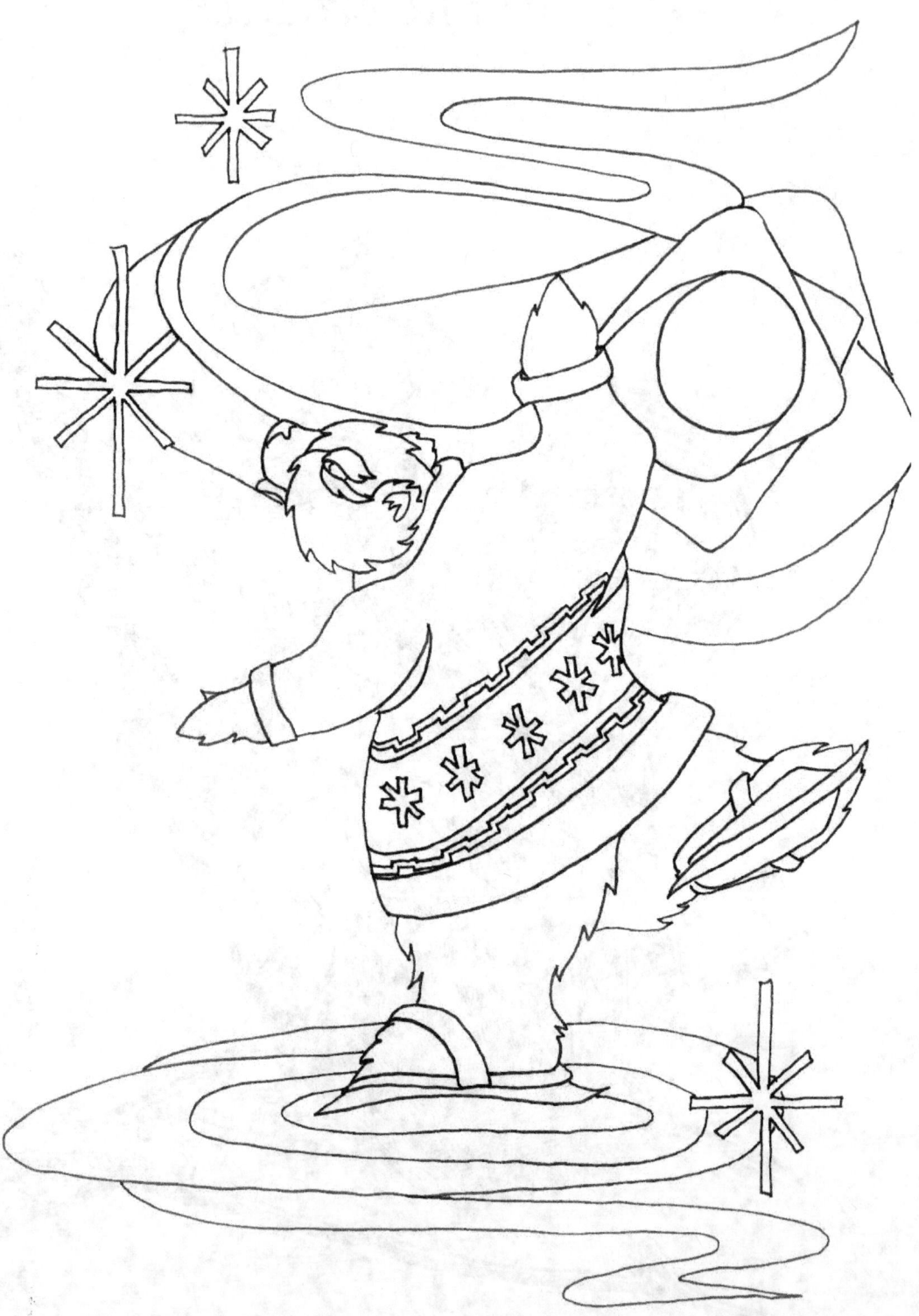

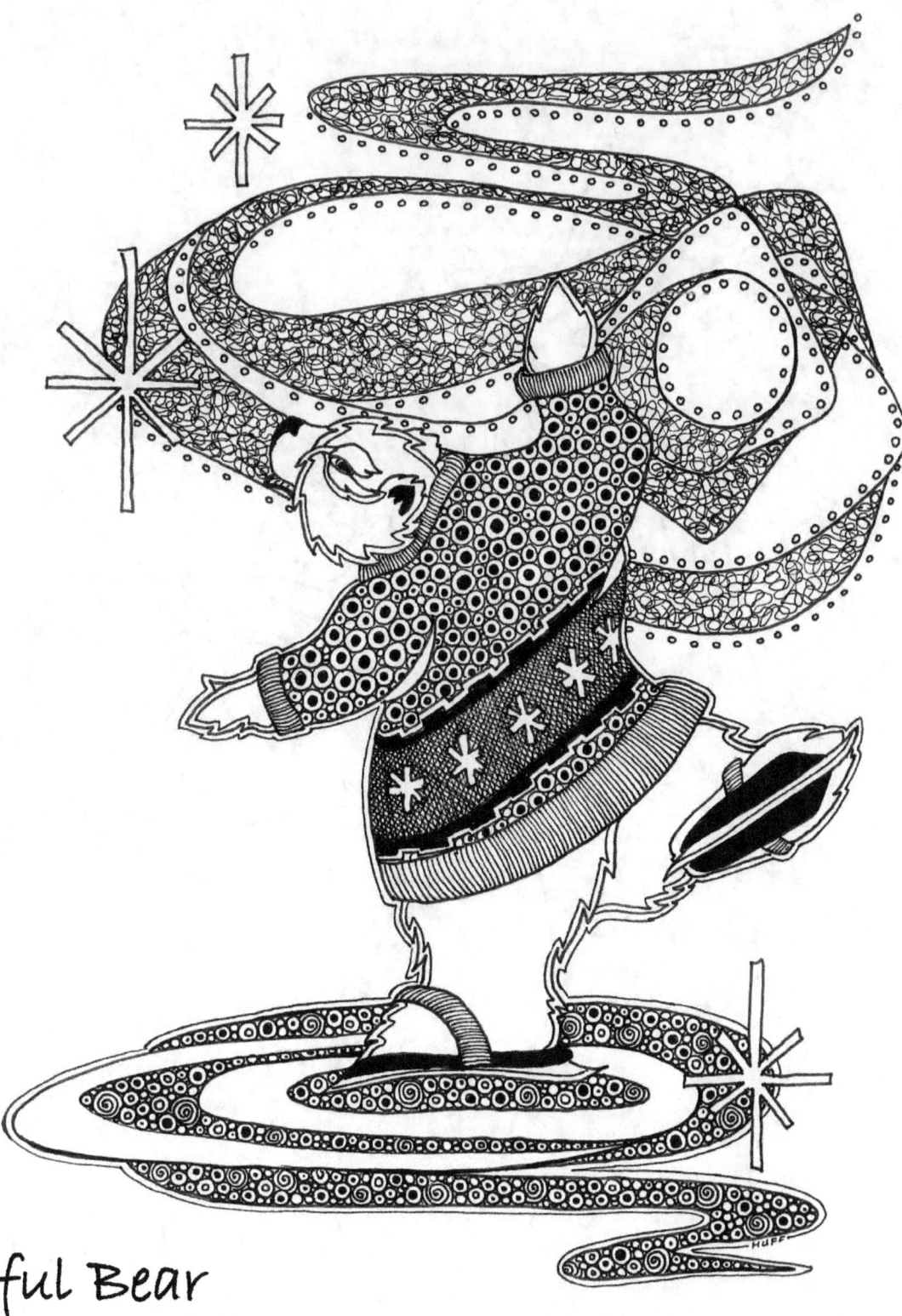

Joyful Bear

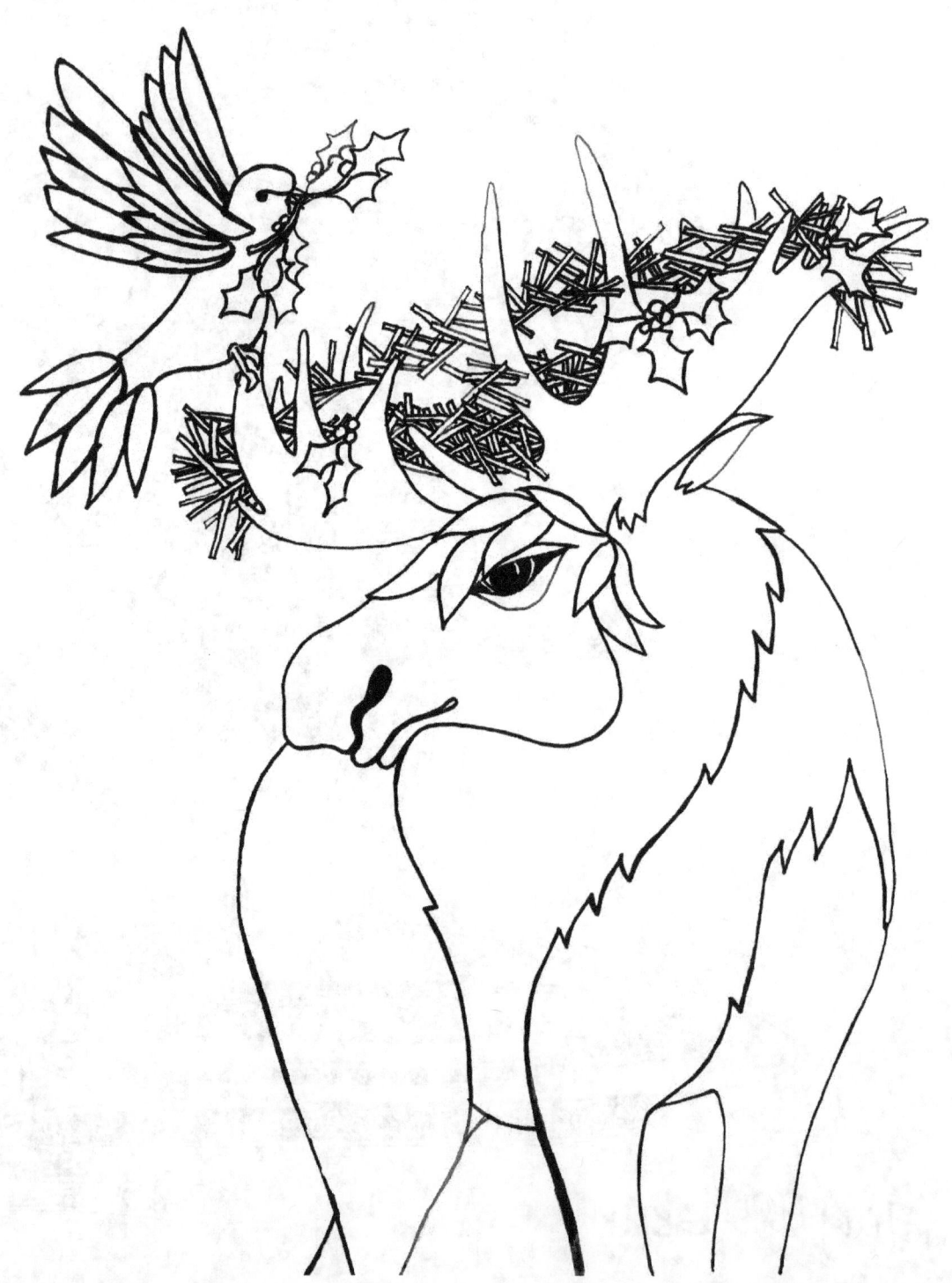

Celebrating with Friends

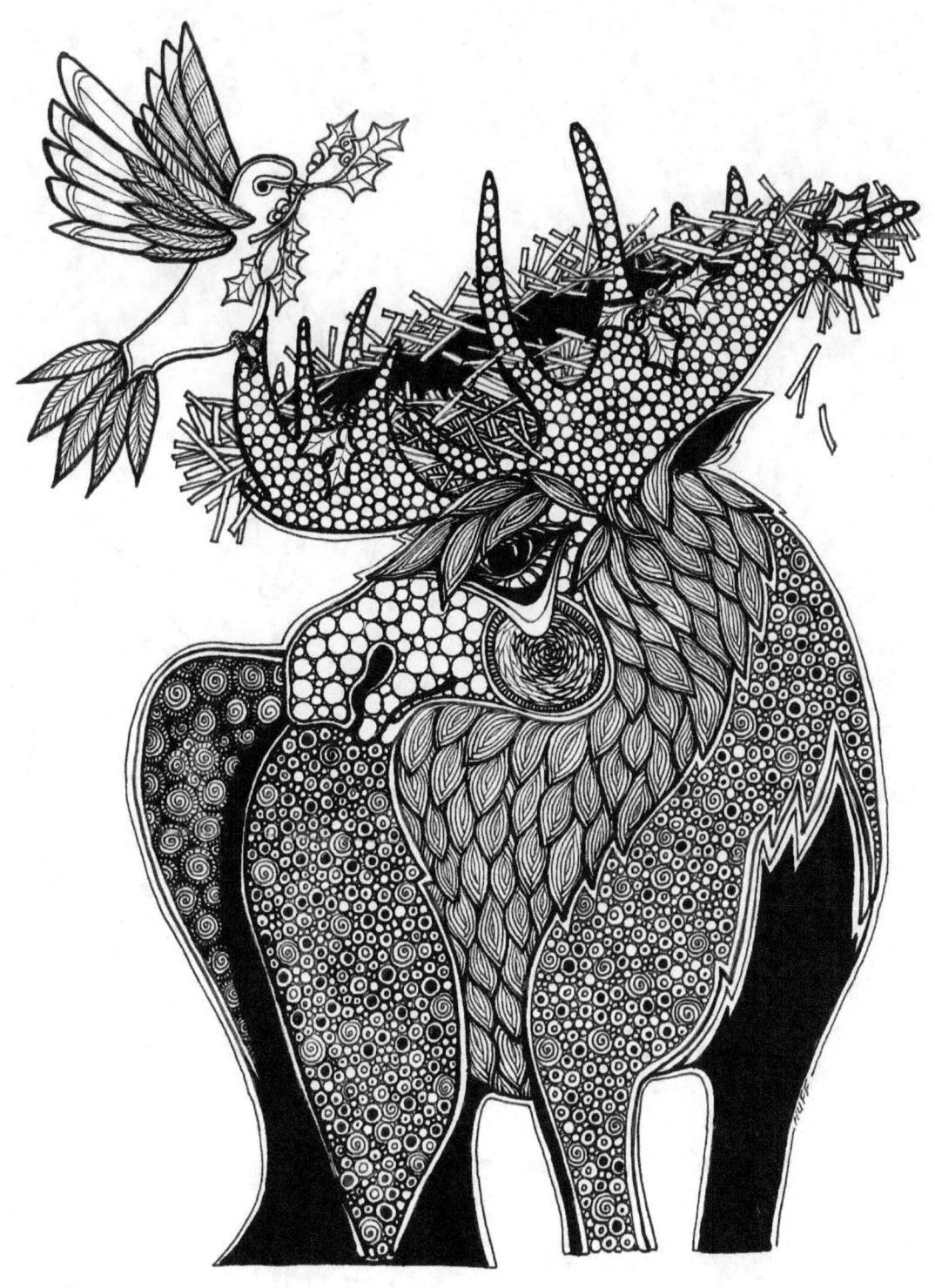

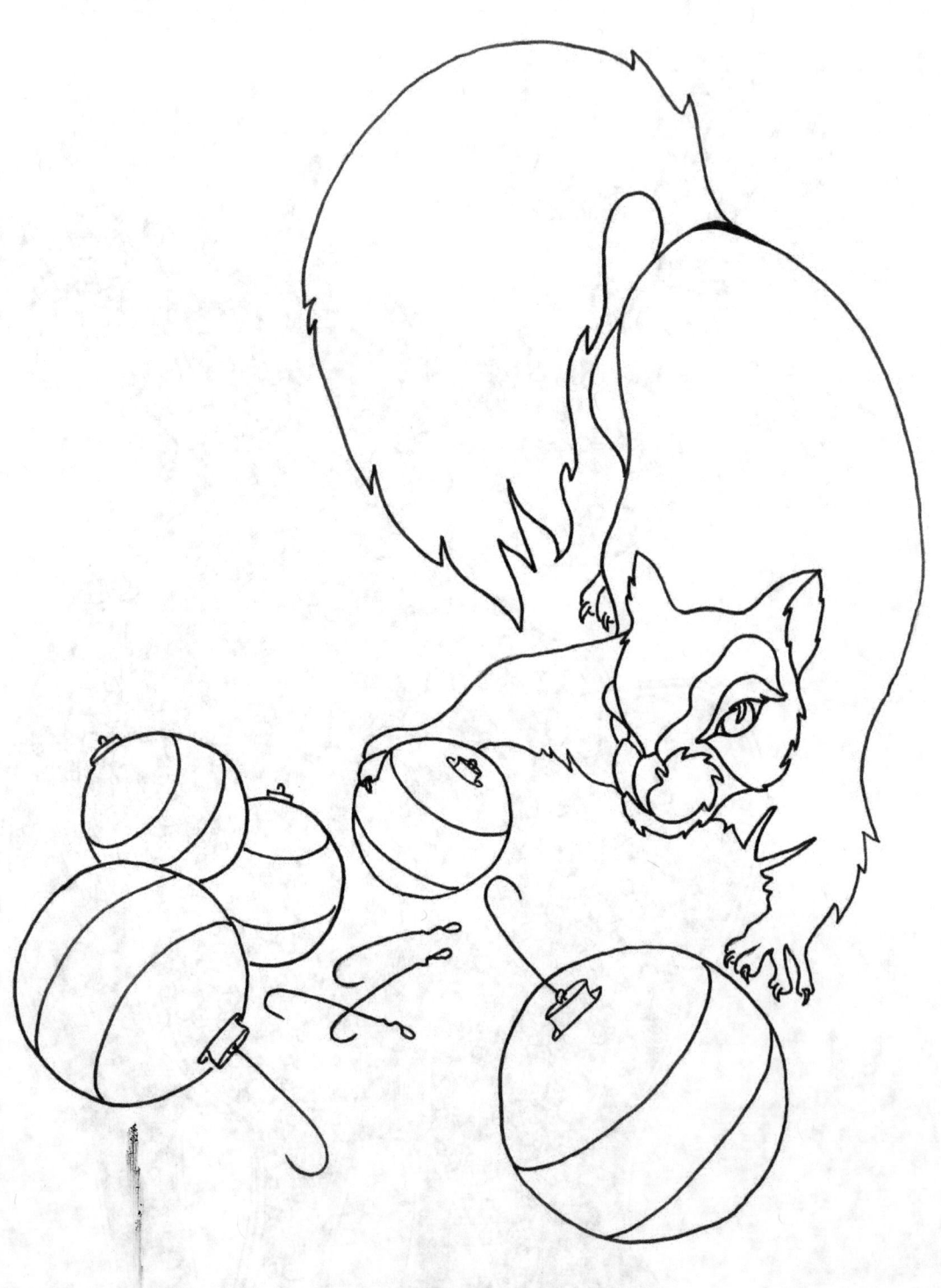

Squirrel
Scramble

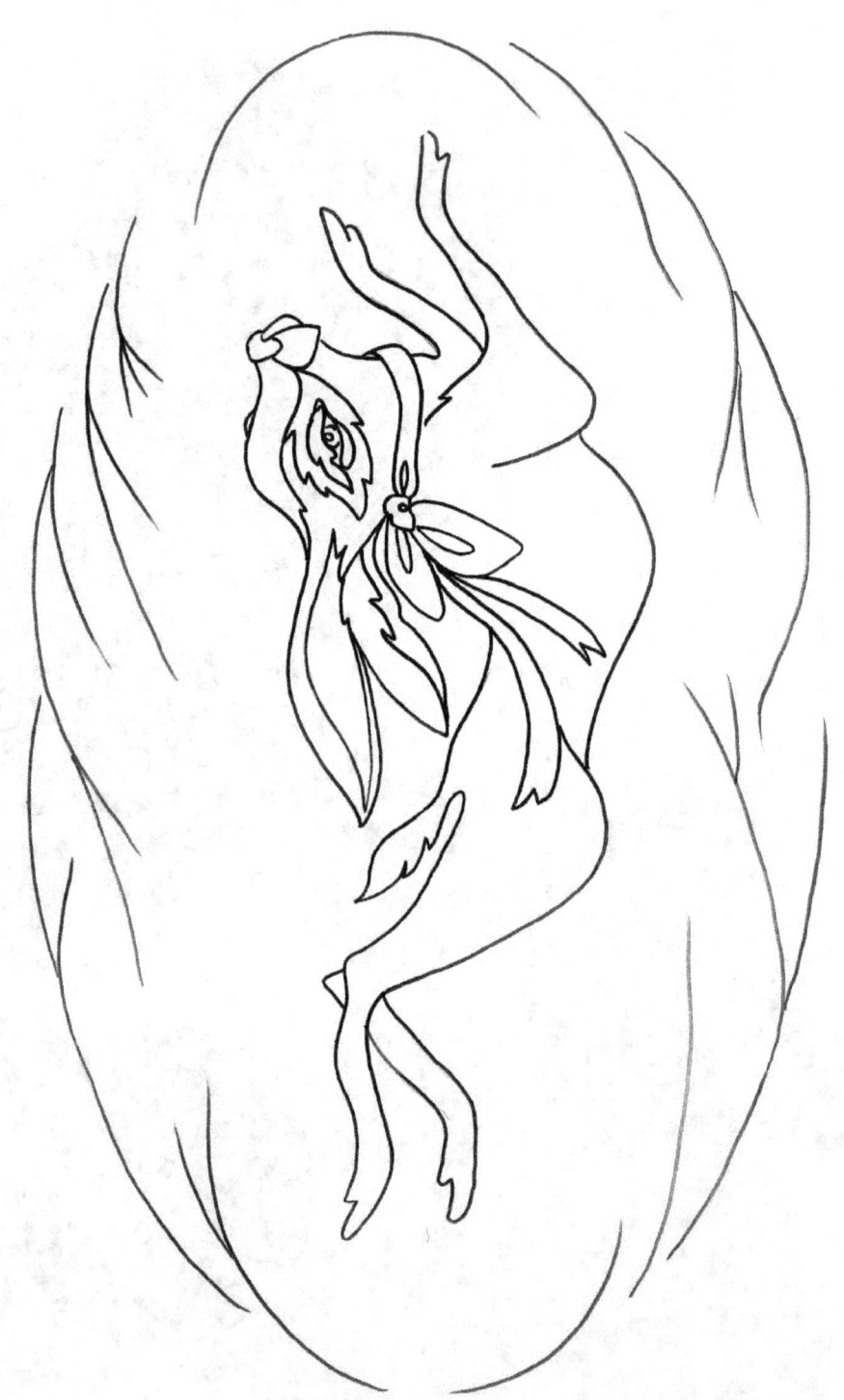

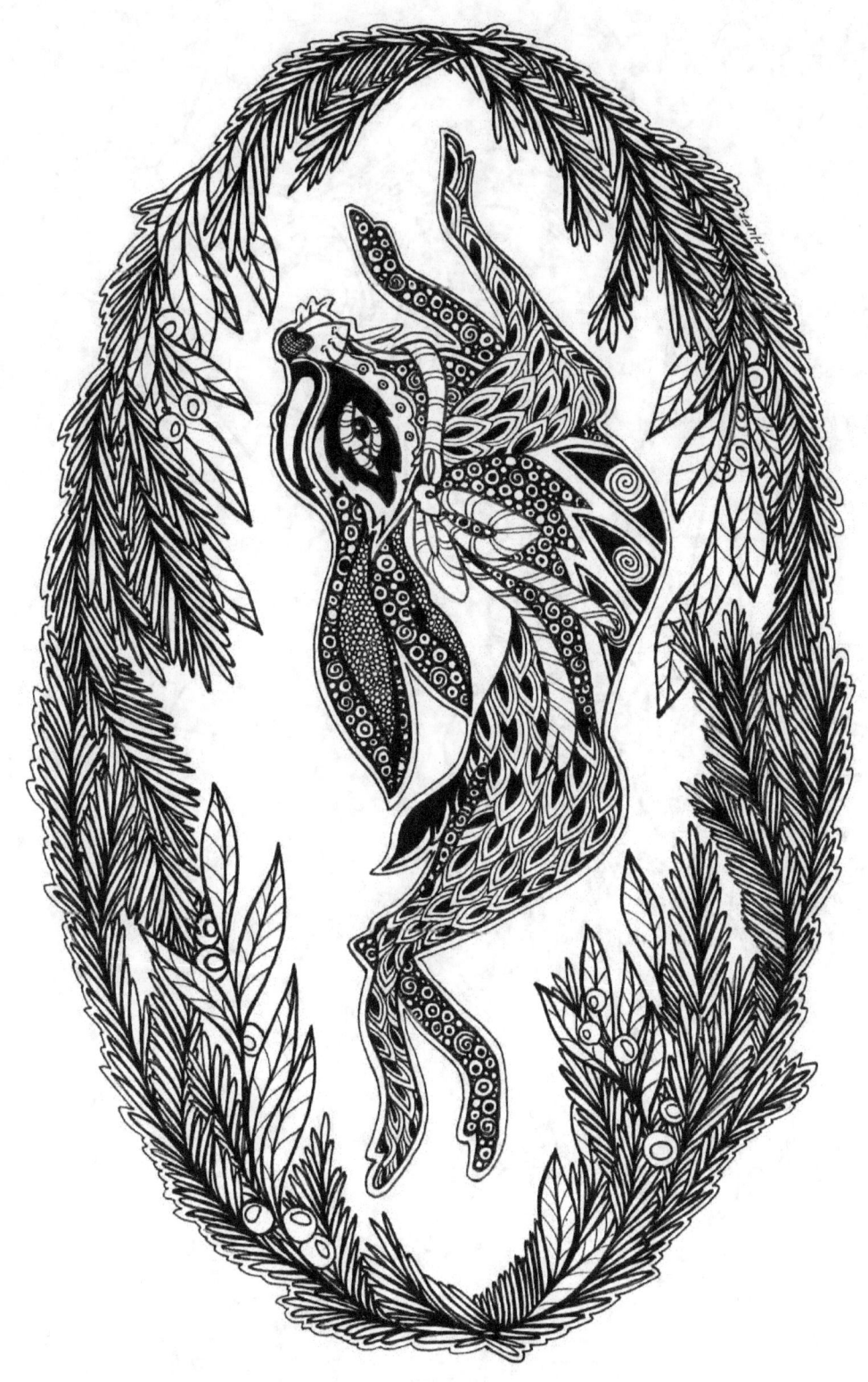

Holiday Hare

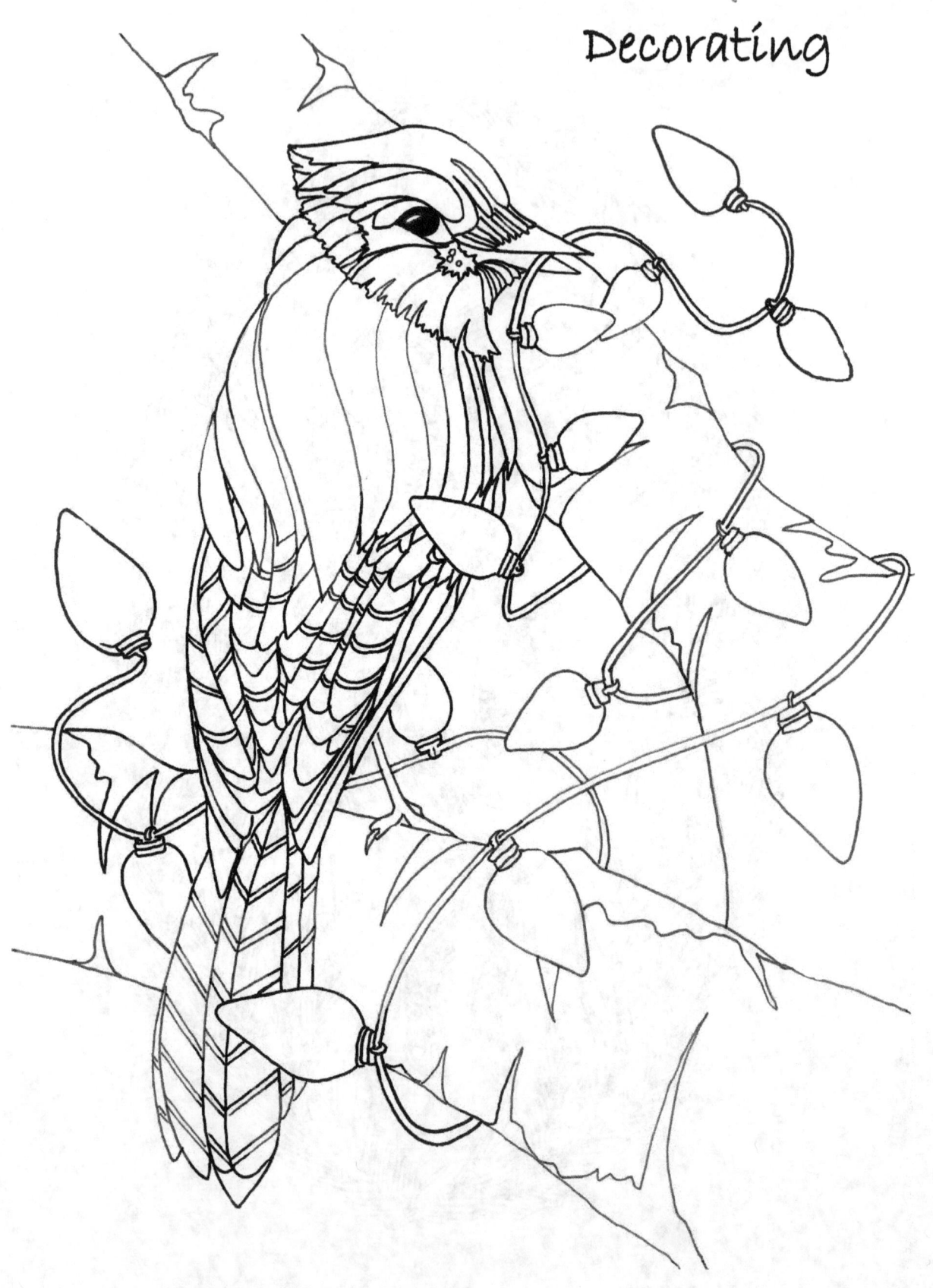

Decorating

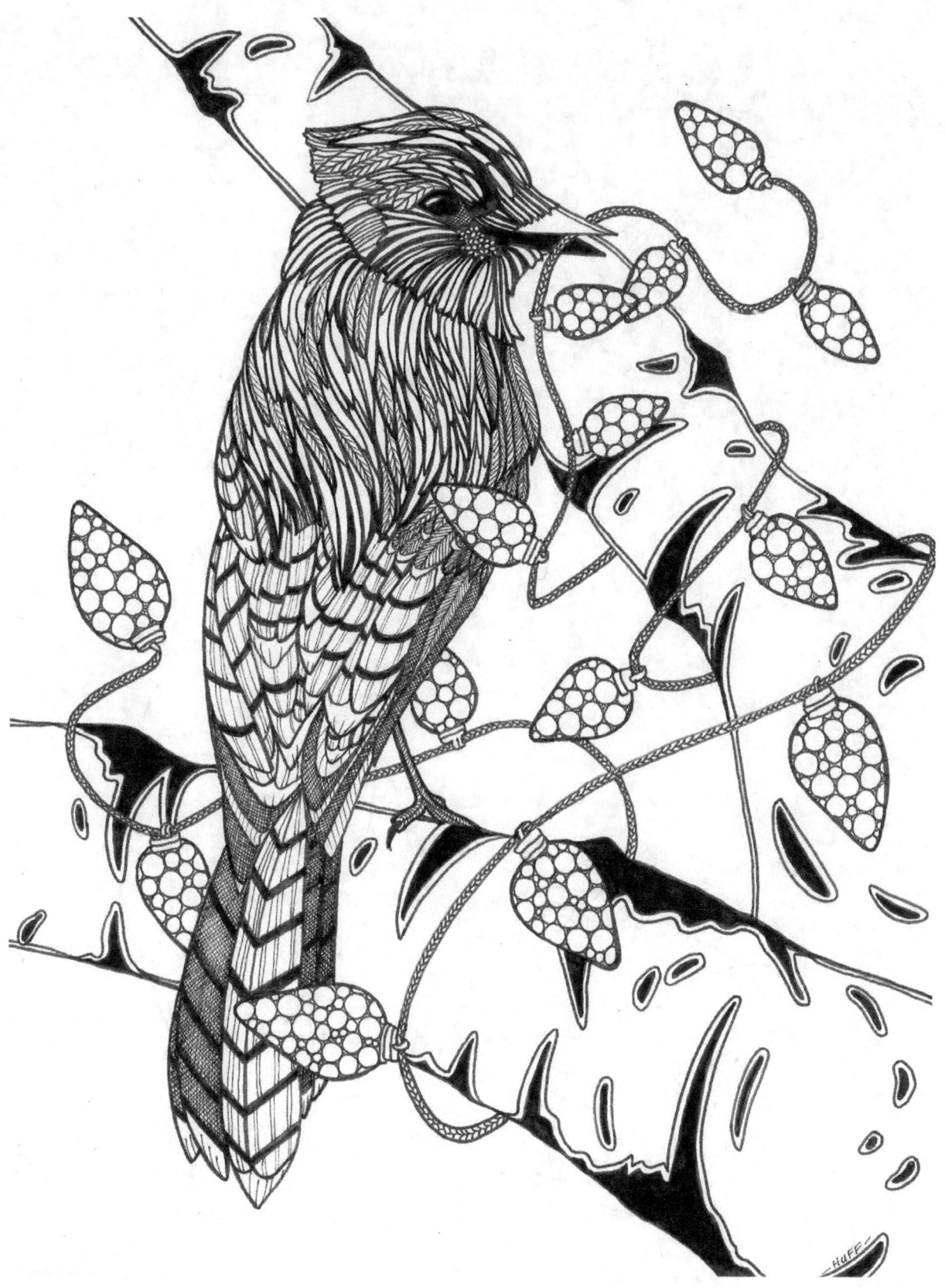

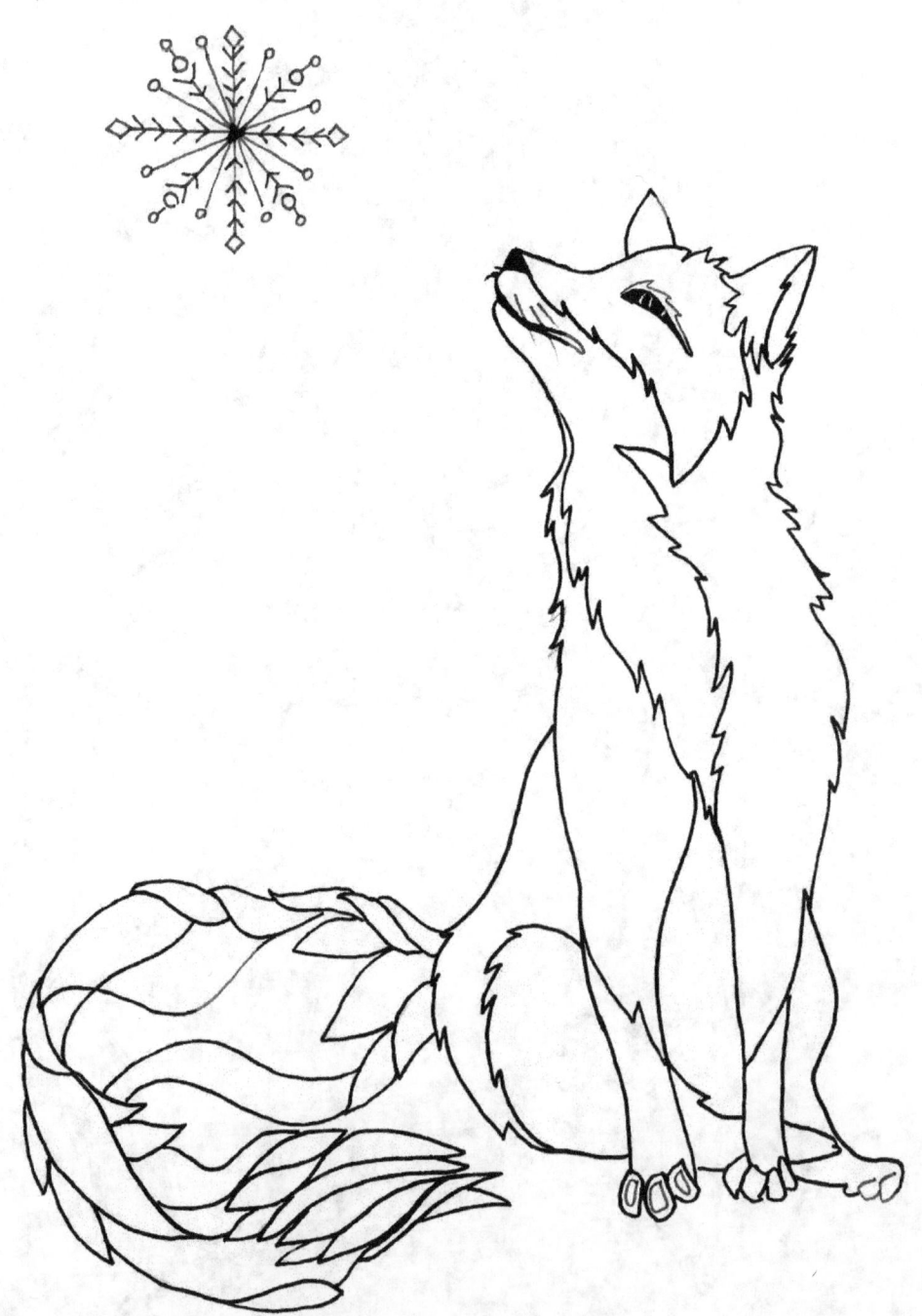

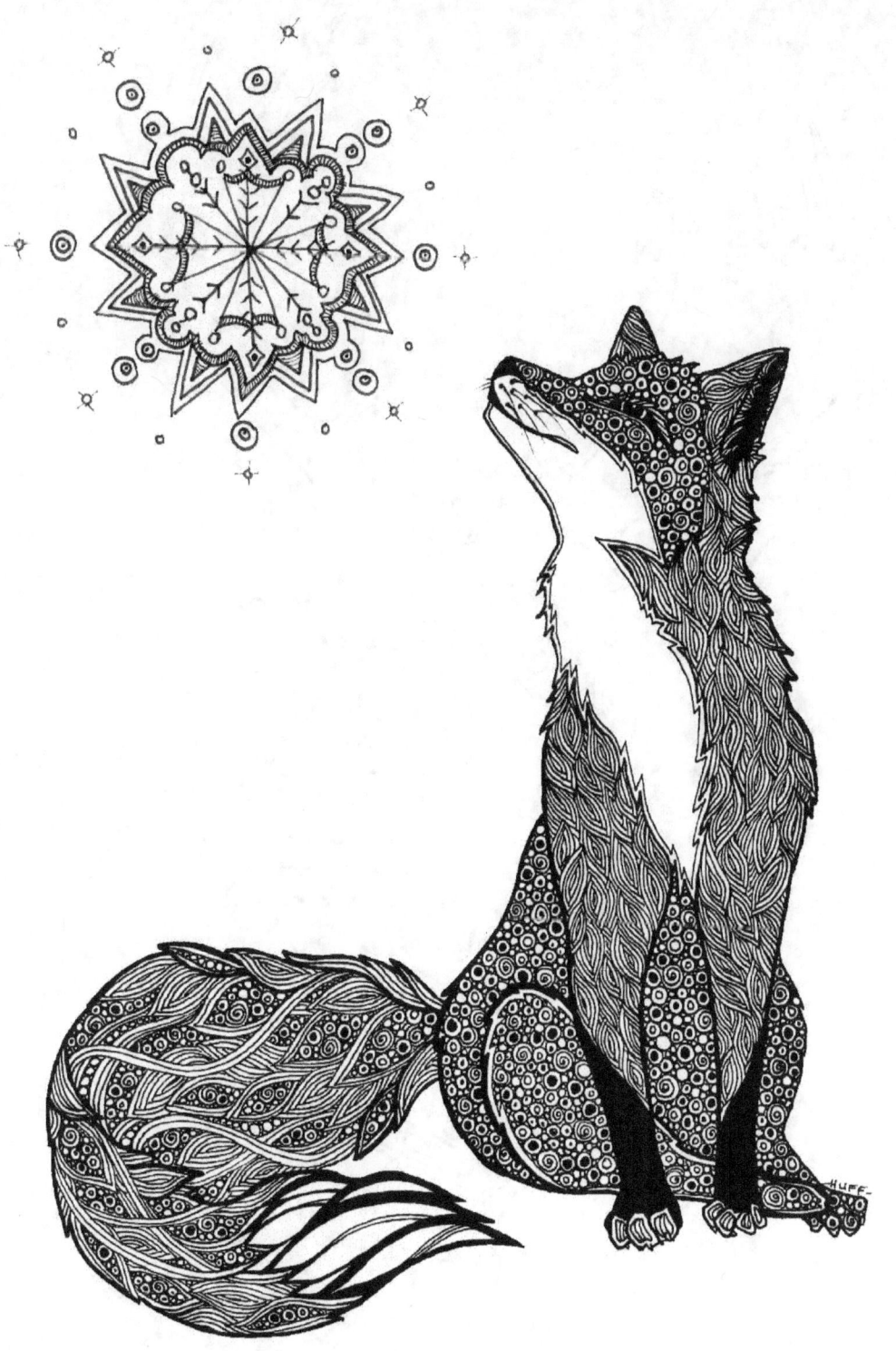

Smiling with Wonder

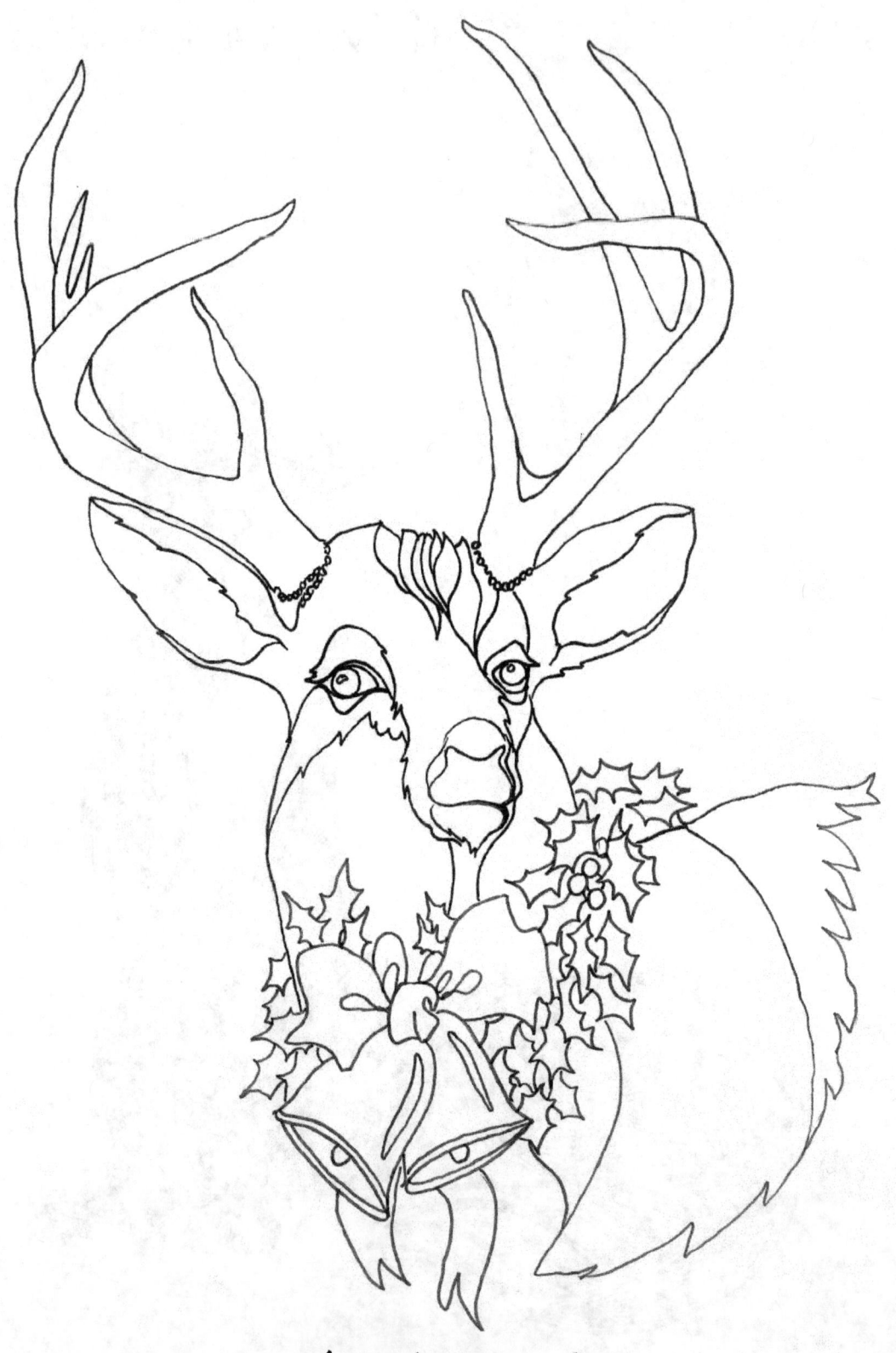

Jingle Buck

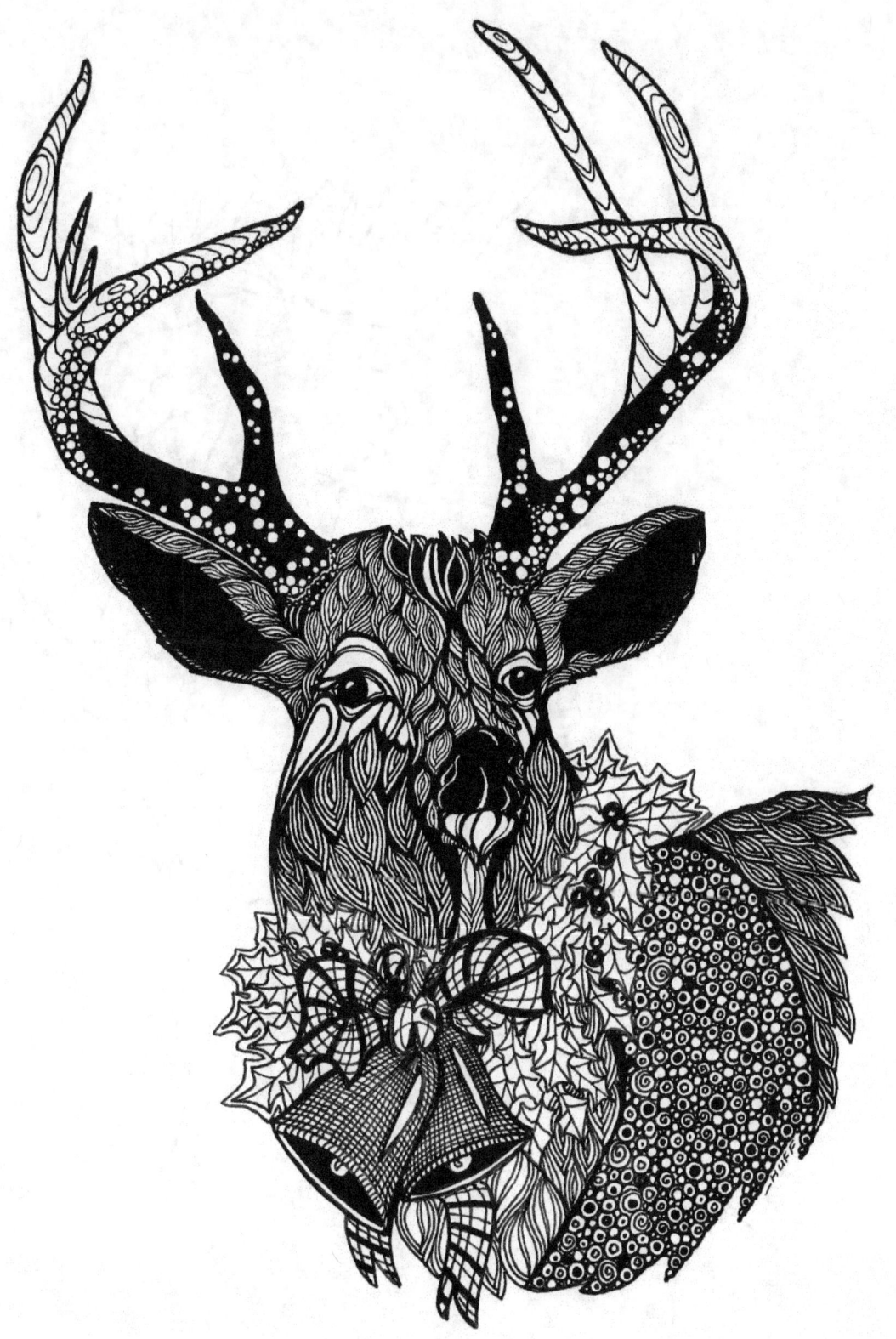

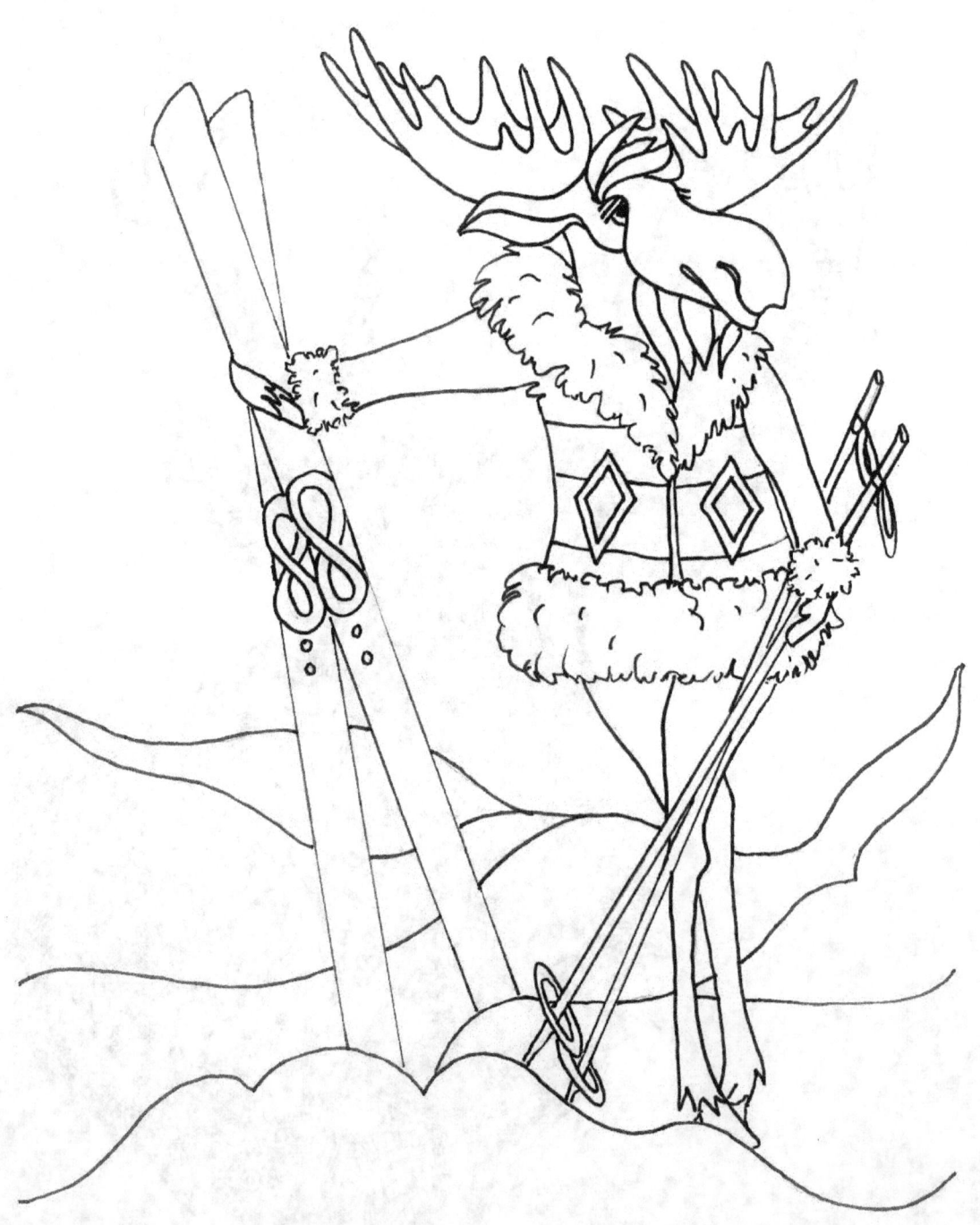

Ski Parka Moose

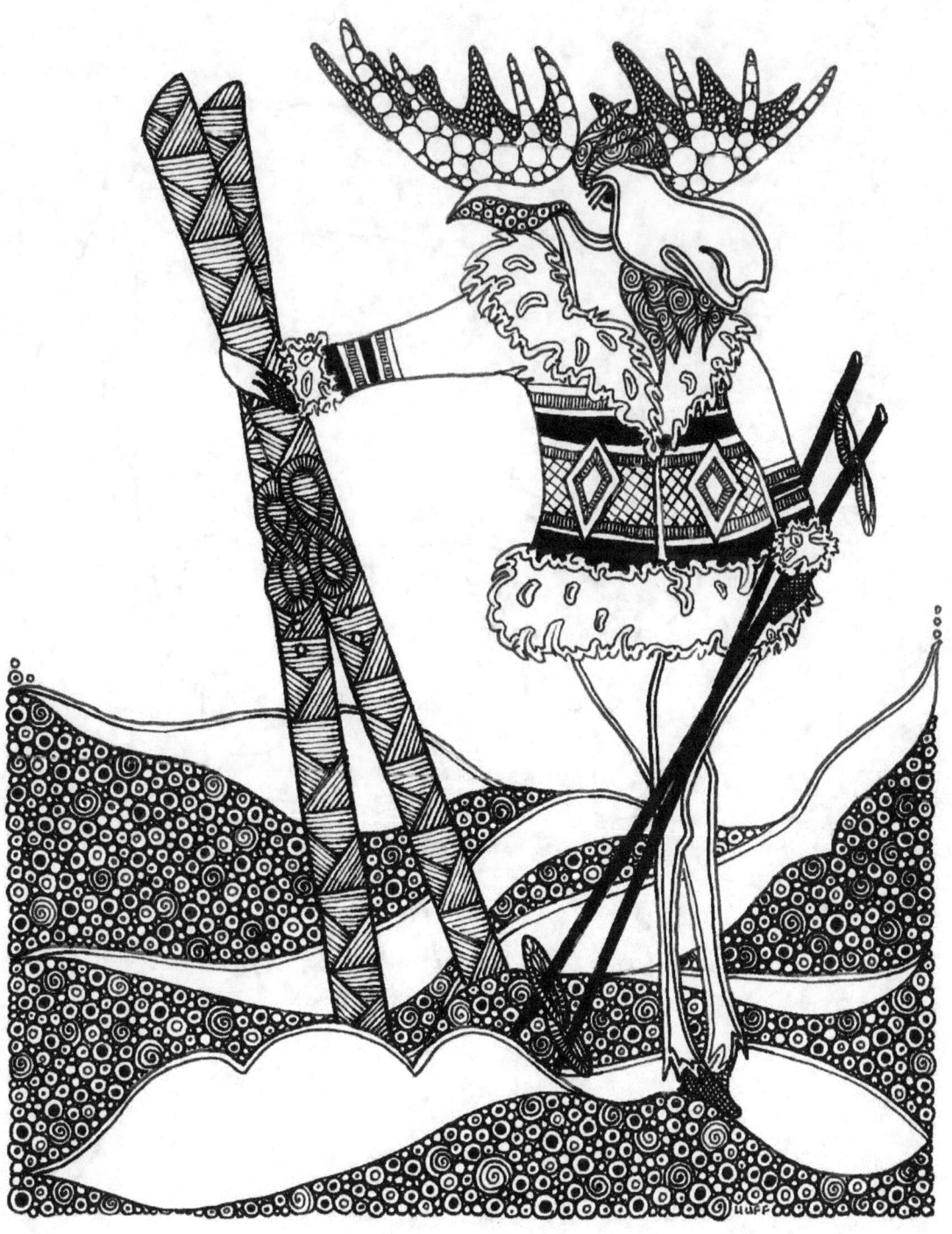

Waiting until Morning

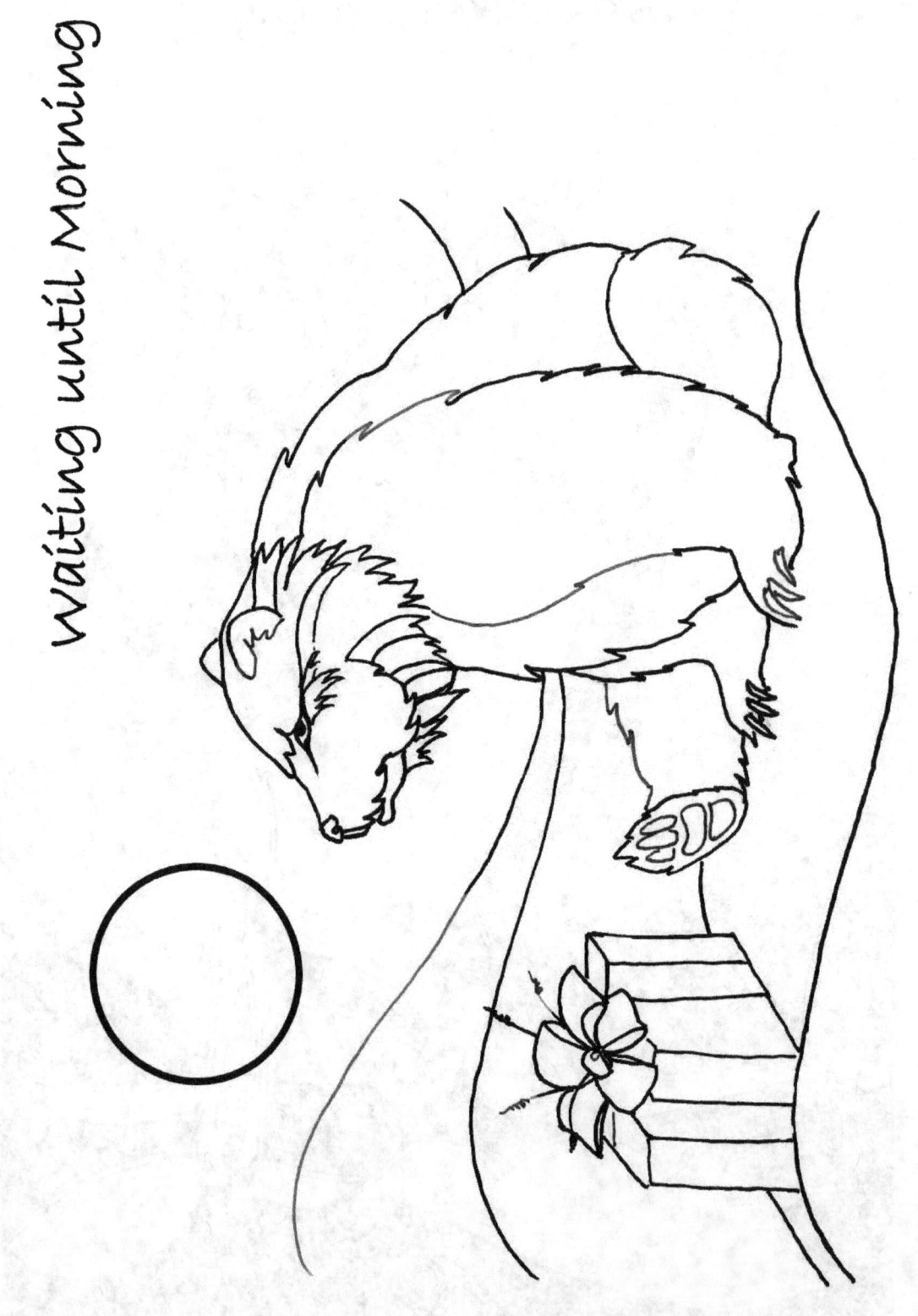

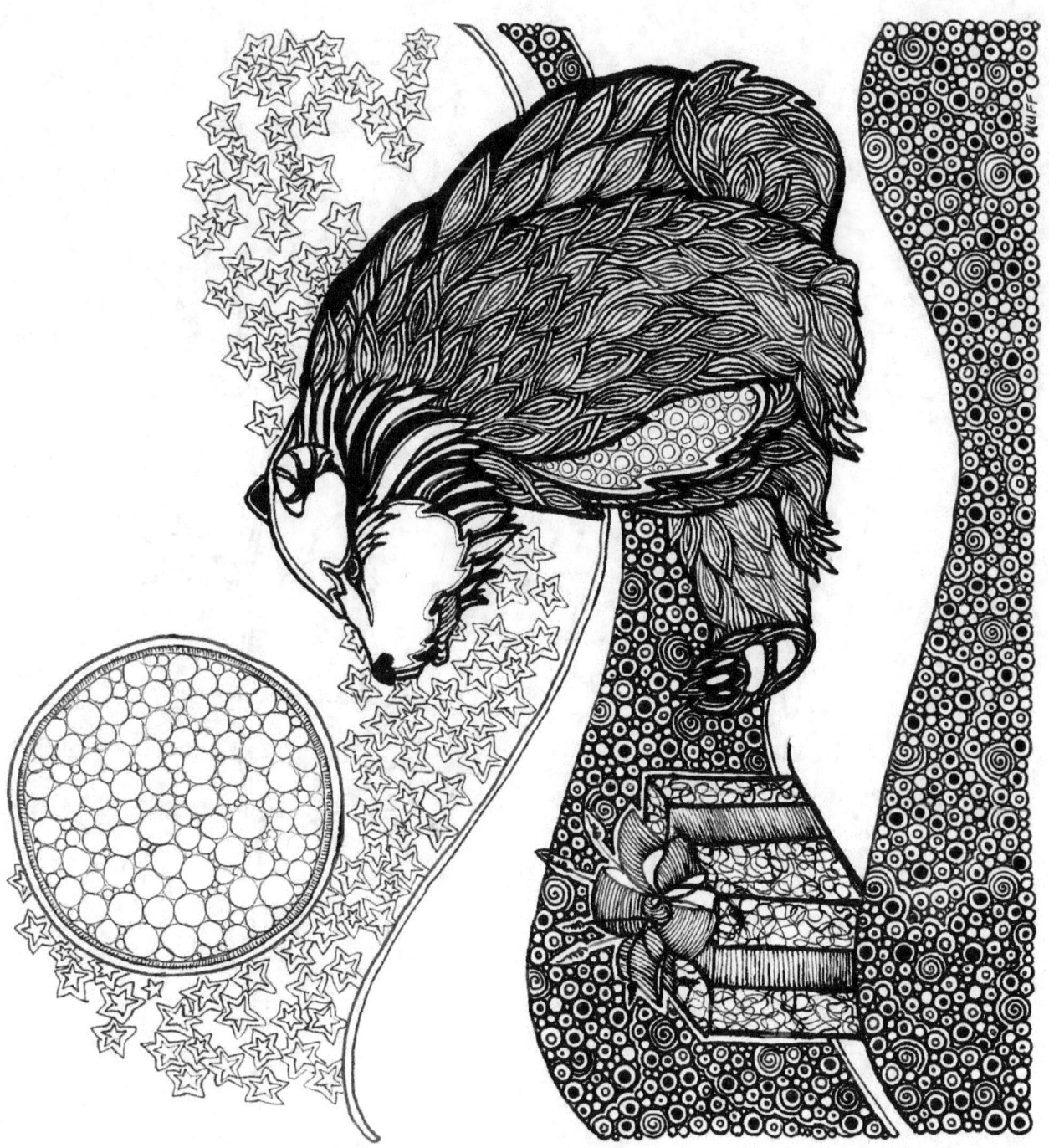

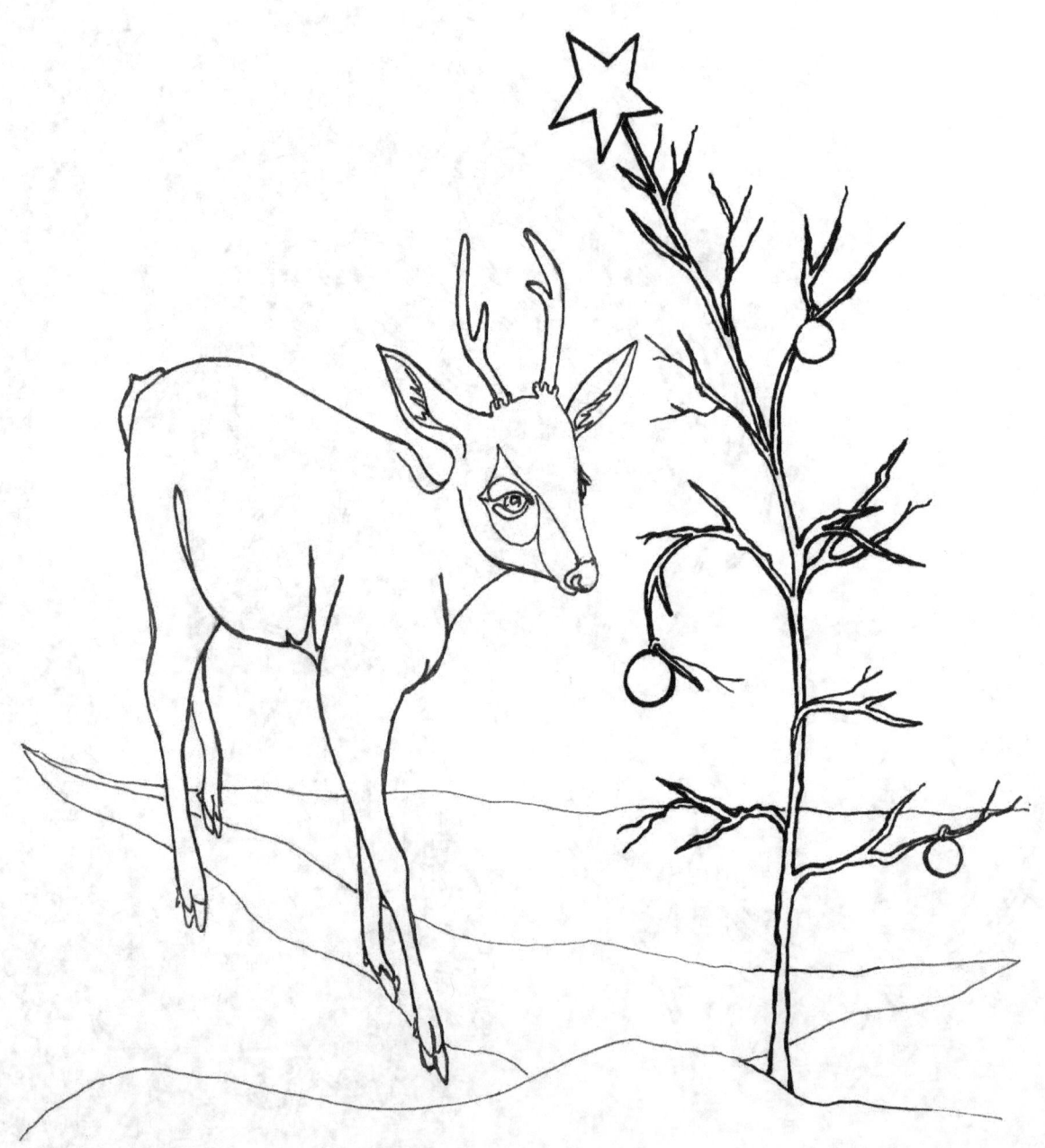

Young Stag

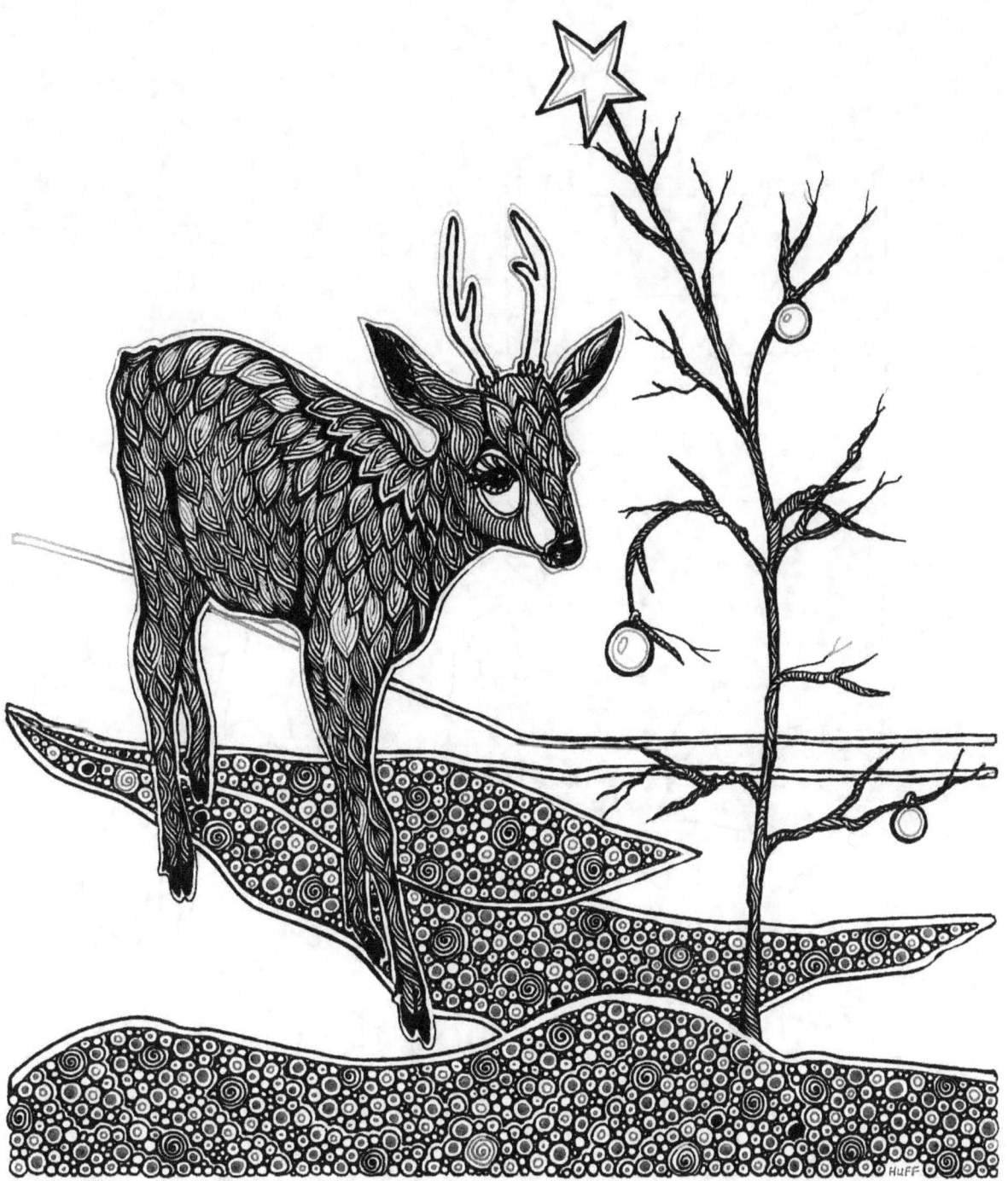

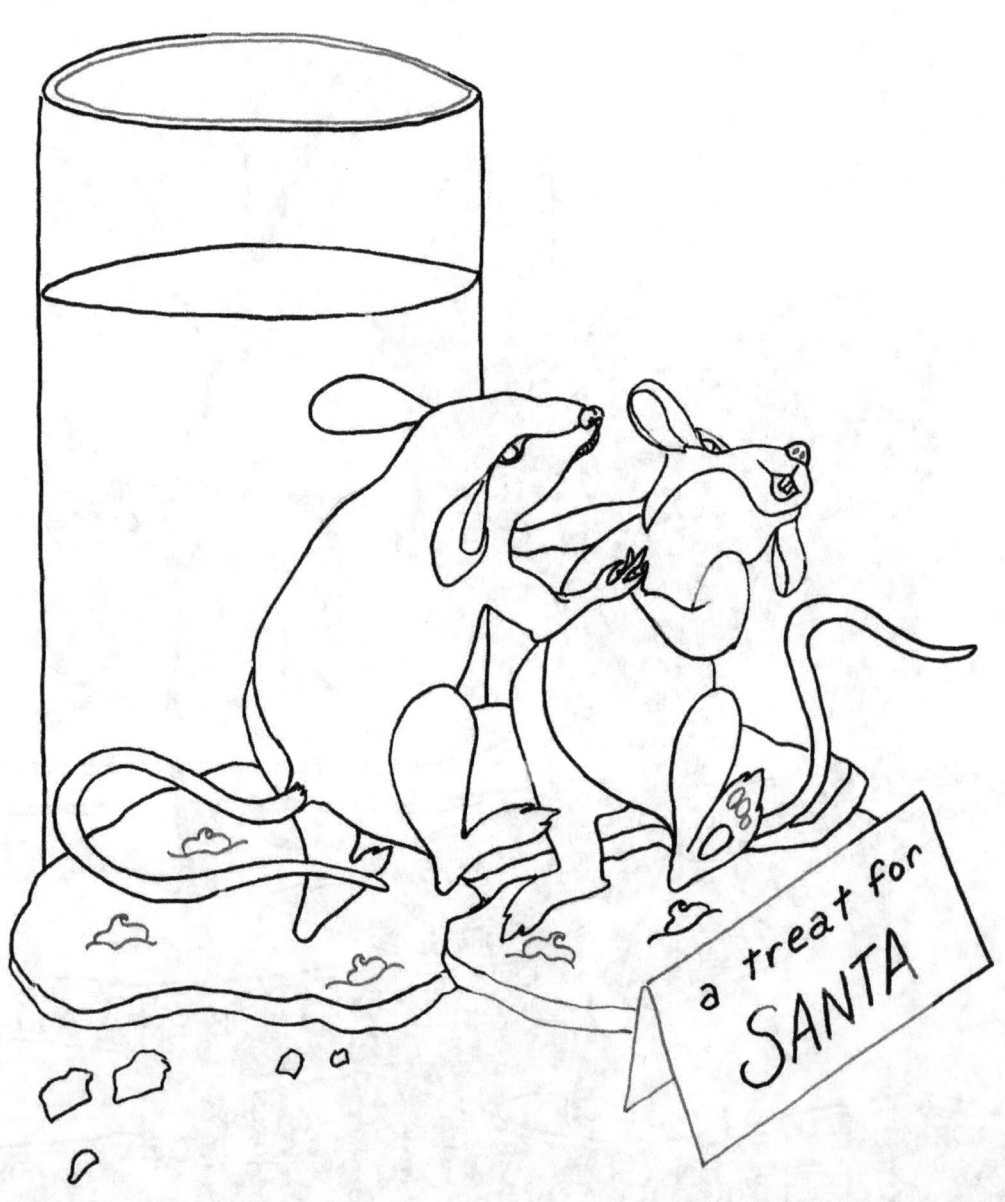

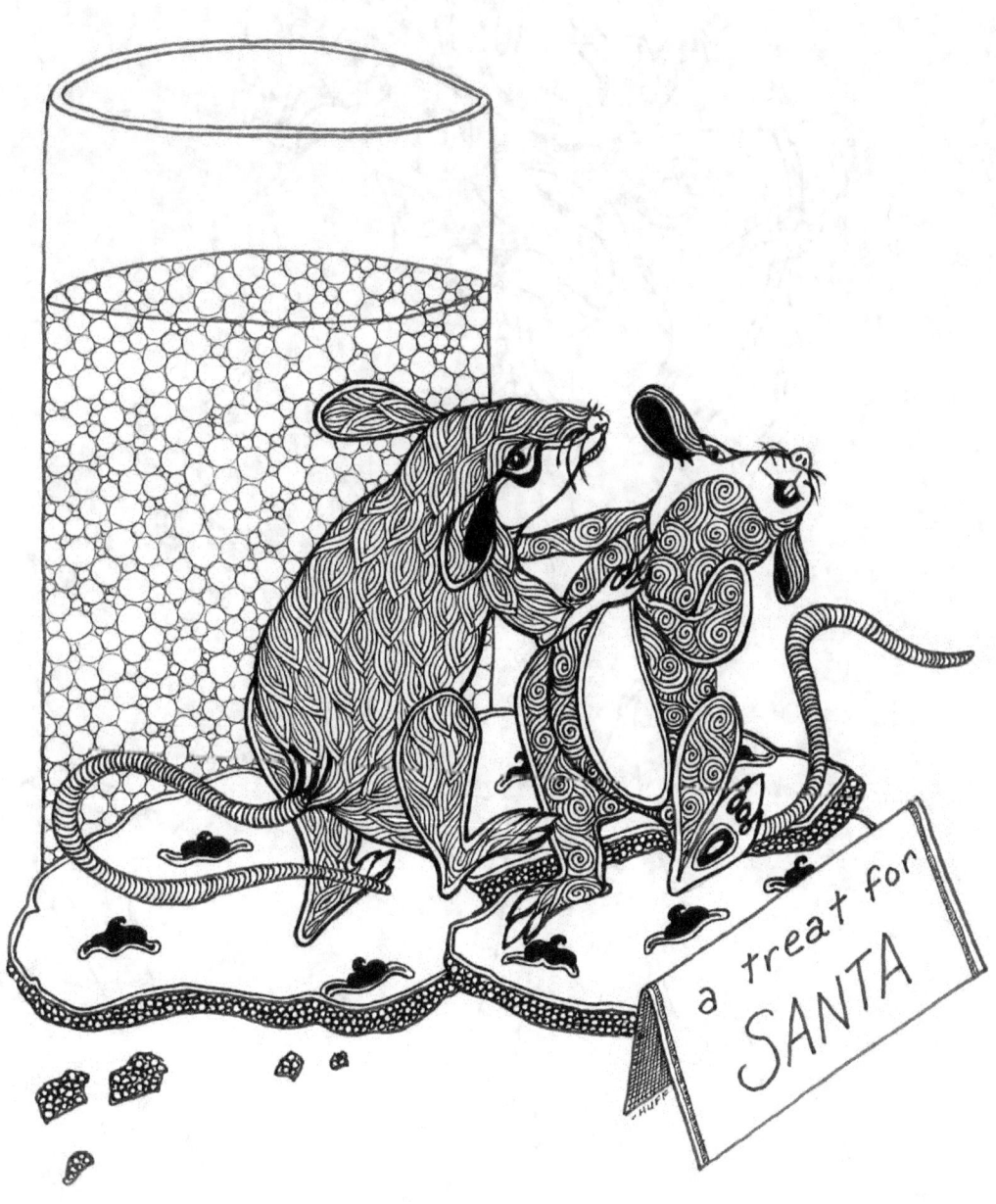

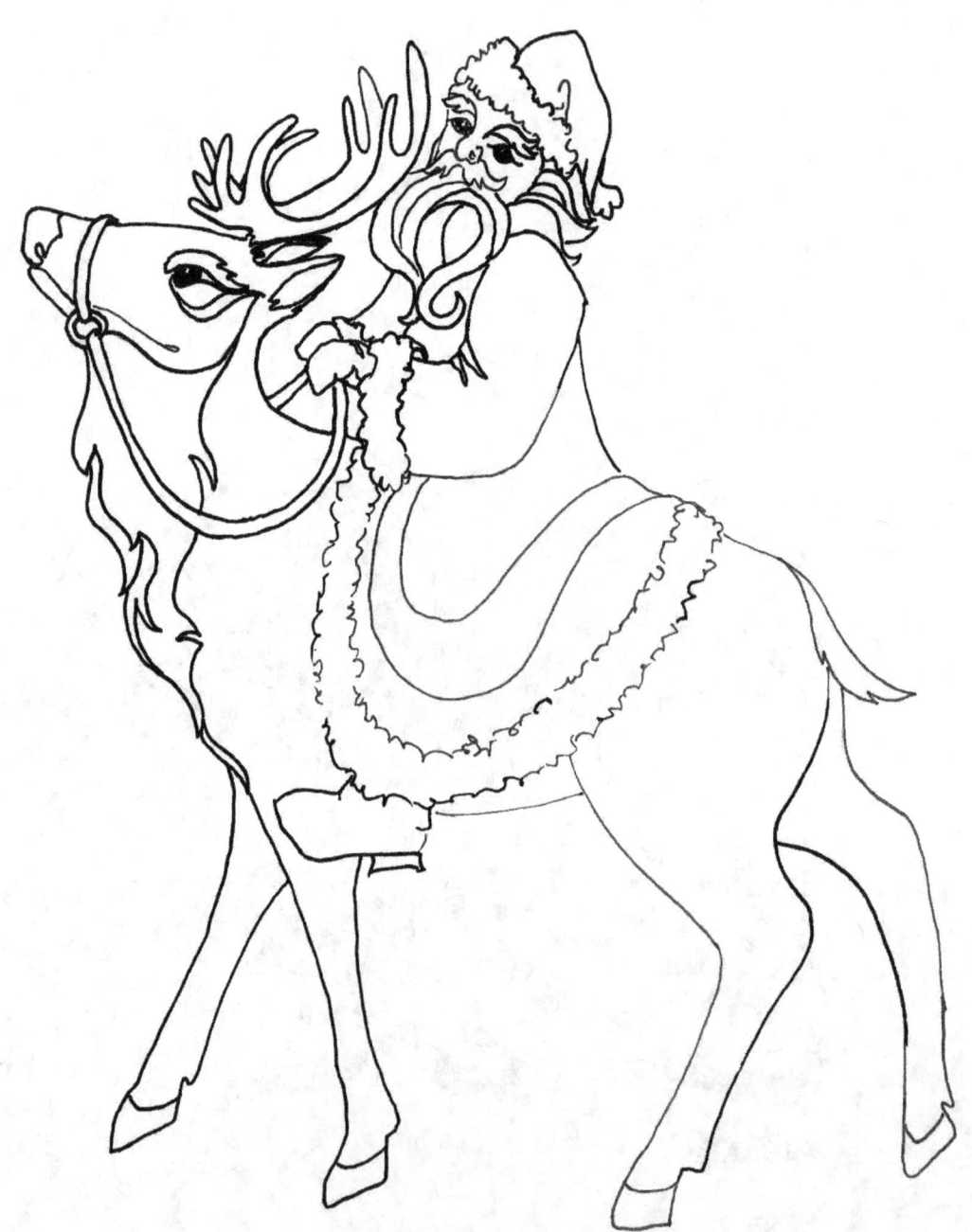

Santa Claus

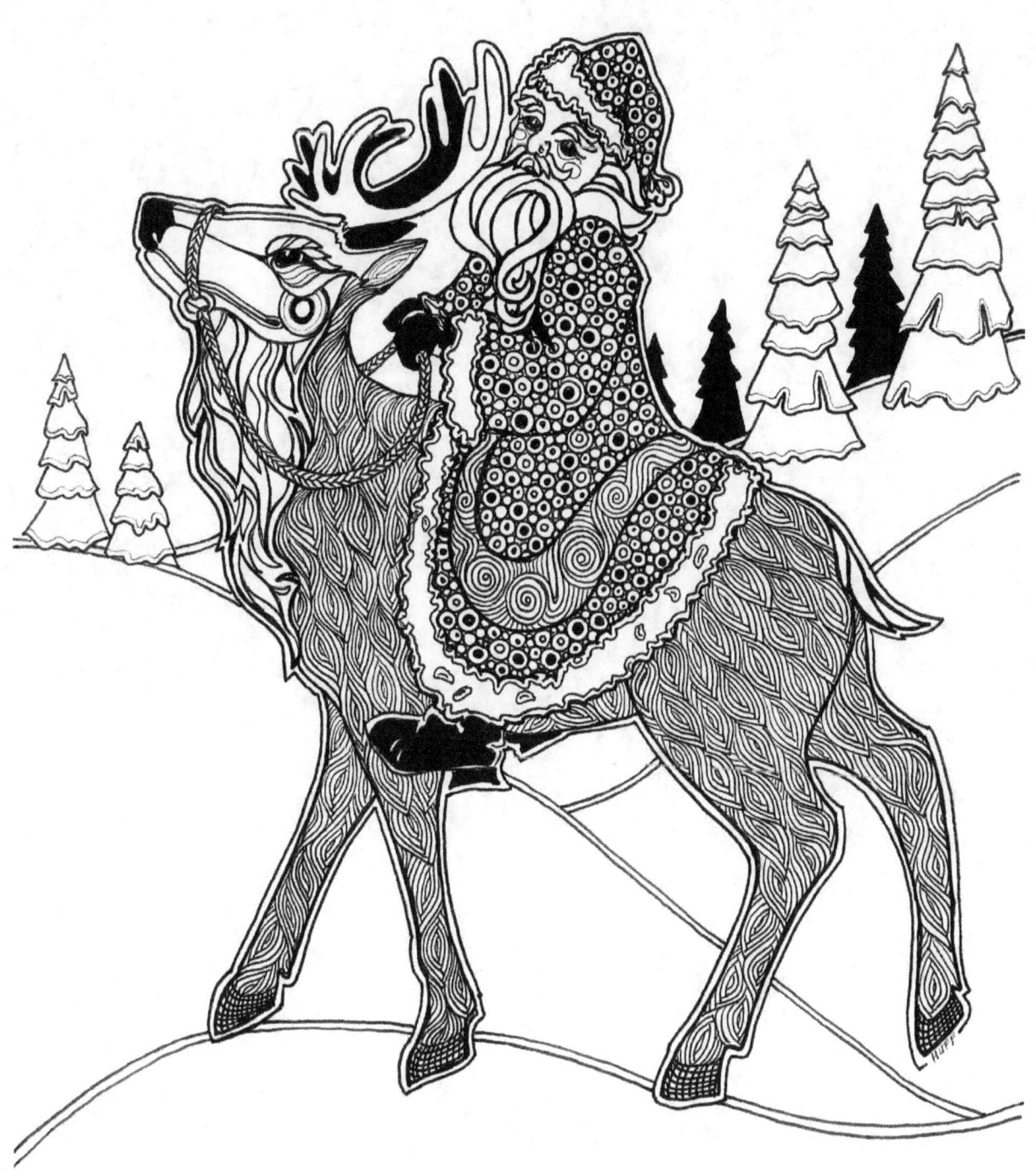